HOW TO FIND A CAREGIVER FOR YOUR LOVED ONE

HOW TO FIND A CAREGIVER FOR YOUR LOVED ONE

Carrie Bruder

Marmont Press
Los Angeles

Published by Marmont Press
Los Angeles, California

Author photograph © 2011 by Jay Bruder
Book design and copyediting by Joey Green
PRINTED IN THE UNITED STATES OF AMERICA

Library of Congress Control Number: 2011916732

ISBN: 0-98-403020-4
ISBN-13: 978-0-9840302-0-0

10 9 8 7 6 5 4 3 2 1

In loving memory of Marilyn

CONTENTS

HOW TO FIND A CAREGIVER

Soon after my wedding, my mother-in-law, Marilyn, offered to help me by returning some china to the department store for a refund. Unable to find a salesperson to assist her, she simply placed the china on the counter in the department store and left.

We took Marilyn to a reputable team of doctors to evaluate her condition. They started with the tests at 8:30 A.M. and finished around 5:30 P.M.

The doctors diagnosed her as being depressed in her marriage. Her second husband, Dick, knew something more substantial was wrong. Marilyn got progressively worse. She developed a second, entirely different personality, which she named "Skippy." Her eyes would bulge and she would speak in a deep, harsh voice. Skippy loved glitter and flashy clothing. Dick found a neurologist, who insisted that Marilyn had something wrong with her brain. The doctor was very unsure of himself and did not have much time for our questions. We needed a more experienced specialist. Dick was finally referred to a top-notch neurologist who determined, after several tests, that Marilyn had frontal lobe dementia.

Marilyn was becoming more confused. My husband, Jay, and I had to become Marilyn's conservator to oversee her affairs, and Marilyn insisted on getting a divorce. I arranged the divorce for Marilyn during my ninth month of pregnancy. Marilyn began spending nights at our home because her alter-ego "Skippy" did not want to go home. To make matters worse, after our baby was born, Skippy was jealous of our new baby girl. The doctor finally prescribed medication, which eventually made Skippy go away—and stay away.

The doctor told us that patients with this kind of dementia usually live no more than five years. We were terrified. Jay and I had to find a caregiver to take care of Marilyn. We did not know how to find a caregiver or what to look for when trying to determine who is right for the job. We soon realized that taking care of a loved one is a full time job. Every year Marilyn's mind deteriorated more—to the point where she could no longer make decisions for herself.

Having taken care of Marilyn for more than eleven years and having hired my fair share of caregivers, I decided to write this book to share my experiences to guide you through the process and help you avoid my mistakes.

Chapter 1
GETTING YOUR LOVED ONE'S AFFAIRS IN ORDER

First Things First

Before your loved one loses his capacity for coherent thought, make an appointment with an attorney to help your loved one set up a Will, Living Will, or a Durable Power of Attorney. Establishing a Living Will or a Durable Power of Attorney in advance allows your loved one to decide what should happen to him if he reaches a point where he cannot make decisions for himself. Make an appointment with an attorney to set up a Will, Power of Attorney, or Living Will. Also, consider setting up a trust to prevent probate problems.

When your loved one can no longer manage to care and protect himself, you may need to file to be the conservator. Being the legal conservator allows you to make arrangements for your loved one's needs, such as meals, transportation, health care, housekeeping, personal care, activities, and clothing. As conservator of the estate, you also manage your loved one's complete finances. There are three different types of conservatorships: General, Limited, and Temporary. General conservatorship is conservator of your loved one's person and estate. Limited conservatorship is for your loved one who needs "limited" assistance. Temporary Conservatorship is for a loved one who needs assistance immediately.

Preparation Checklist

❑ Set up Will, Living Will, Durable Power of Attorney.

❑ If you are unable to set up a Will, Durable Power of Attorney due to mental capacity of loved one, file for a conservatorship with attorney.

❑ List all of your loved one's assets, partnerships, bank accounts and retirement accounts before he loses his ability to help you do so.

❑ Review your loved one's monthly expenses.

❑ Find out if your loved one has a safety deposit box.

❑ List all mortgage loans and policy numbers.

❏ List all your loved one's health, life and car insurers.

❏ Make copies of your loved one's insurance medical cards.

❏ List all the medications that your loved one is taking and who prescribed the medication. Describe each container, the color and shape of the medication, why your loved one takes the medication, the dosage and the time and day that the medication should be taken, and any possible side effects. Make sure that the description includes the name, address and phone number of the pharmacist and who prescribed the medication.

❏ Prepare an emergency contact list with the names, phone numbers, and addresses of family members, doctors, and hospitals.

❏ Prepare a list of medical problems (heart failure, asthma, etc.) that your loved one has experienced in the past so that they are aware and will know what to do in certain emergencies.

Finding the Right Doctor

If your loved one is unhappy with her doctor, or if your loved one does not have a doctor, interview doctors yourself. If you need to find a doctor, ask a friend, family member or other doctor to refer you to someone. Your loved one will need a general practitioner and also someone who specializes in her particular illness. A friend or co-worker who has a family member with a similar condition may be able to refer you to a doctor. Make sure that you check the doctor's credentials and find out if the doctor accepts Medicare. Medicare has a toll free number that can assist you finding Medicare approved doctors.

Interview the doctor and bring your loved one with you. Make sure that that your loved one and the doctor get along and understand each other. Ask for the doctor's work hours. Some doctors only work certain hours, which may not be convenient for you and your loved one. Make sure that the doctor respects your loved one's wishes regarding death. You need a doctor who understands and respects your loved one's wishes.

When you arrive at the Doctor's office you should have all insurance cards (private insurance, Medicare) and a copy of your loved one's medical records. If you are switching doctors, call your previous doctor and have her send over your loved one's files to the new doctor so the new doctor can review the case history before the exam and prescribe the appropriate medication, if necessary.

■ Bring all of your loved one's medications with you, including any vitamins. Certain medications cannot be taken with vitamins.

■ Inform the doctor of any past surgeries and or illnesses your loved one has or experienced.

■ Inform the doctor about your loved one's eating habits, sleeping patterns, and bowel movements.

■ Inform the doctor of any eyeglasses, dentures, limbs, hearing aids, or any other devices.

■ If your loved one can talk and understand the questions that are being addressed, allow your loved one to talk and answer the questions. If your loved one neglects to give any information, then offer that information only.

■ Get a second opinion. Doctors do make mistakes and different doctors have different opinions. If you do not understand what the doctor is telling you, inform him that you are not familiar with this illness, ask him to explain it to you, and ask for literature on the illness. Do not be embarrassed to ask.

■ If your loved one is diagnosed with an illness and does not understand what is happening, elect one family member to communicate with the doctor. Having several family members continually calling the doctor and asking about the prognosis will only infuriate the doctor and may cause more harm than good. One family member will find out what the doctor has to say and relay that information to the rest of the family. You could end up in a very confusing situation if more than one family member is involved in dealing with the doctor.

Chapter 2
KEEPING YOUR LOVED ONE AT HOME

Before hiring a caregiver, you'll have to make the appropriate preparations for keeping your loved one at home.

Valuables

Remove all valuables from the home including all jewelry, paintings, china and items with sentimental value to your family. Place valuable jewelry in a safety deposit box. If your loved one insists on having jewelry, buy inexpensive costume jewelry. Do not tell your loved one or the caregiver that it is fake.

Clothing

Use permanent marking pen to label all clothing on the inside of the garment with your loved one's name to avoid any possible confusion. Continually take inventory of the clothing in the presence of your caregiver to make certain no clothing has mysteriously disappeared and to let the caregiver know that you are doing so.

Safety

A loved one suffering from dementia may do things to inhibit the safety of his well being. Just as you would safety-proof your home for a child, you need to safety-proof your home for an adult who needs assistance. You will need to eliminate potential dangers from the home. Crawl on the floor and treat the situation as if your loved one is a curious infant.

■ Get special lock covers for the stove, oven, and other appliances.

■ Install the proper grab bars in the bathroom and apply decals to slippery surfaces where needed.

■ Provide plastic or paper cups in the bathroom instead of breakable drinking glasses.

■ Place safety covers in all electrical sockets.

■ Remove matches from the home.

■ Remove hazardous cleaning supplies that contain chemicals.

■ Lock all medication in a cabinet that cannot be accessed by your loved one. A person who is not

My Experience
I Thought It Was Mine

Marilyn owned an abundance of sweaters, shoes, and beautiful purses. Unfortunately, caregivers stole more than half of her sweaters, most of her shoes, and all of her nice purses. I would often see the caregiver wearing one of Marilyn's sweaters. The caregiver would claim the sweater belonged to her.

in his right mind may think he needs medication when the caregiver is using the bathroom.

■ Remove sharp items such as metal nail filers, scissors, knifes, and razors.

■ Make sure the home is well lit to create an environment that is happy and bright, not dark and depressing. (Be sure to check with the doctor first to make sure the illness does not require low light).

■ The Grossman Burn Center in Sherman Oaks, California, suggests adjusting the temperature on the water heater to 98.6 degrees Fahrenheit. Like a child, your loved one could burn herself if she adjusts the water temperature while the caregiver turns her back momentarily to grab a towel. The elderly and children have thinner, more sensitive skin that can easily be burned.

■ Remove all loose area rugs to prevent your loved one from tripping and seriously injuring himself. If your loved one insists on having area rugs in the home, place different colored rugs in the entry ways over a rubber pad to help alert your loved one to nearby steps.

■ Walk around the perimeter of the home and remove anything that might cause injury or create a danger for your loved one.

■ If your loved one has dementia, consider installing a bolted lock on the outside doors to prevent her from running away.

■ Provide the caregiver with several copies of a phone list laminated on a card for the house, the car, your loved one's wallet, and for the caregiver's wallet. List your the numbers for your home phone, work phone, cellular phone, pager, and the number of someone else if you cannot be reached in an emergency.

■ On the back of the laminated phone card include a photo of your loved one. If the security at the mall, for example, needs to know what your loved one looks like, your caregiver will be able to provide that picture.

■ Provide a list of your loved one's medications, the doses of each medication, and the hours the medication will need to be given.

■ Provide a list of all doctors and their specialties. Give the address, phone, and emergency numbers for all doctors.

■ Provide gloves for the caregiver (for changing undergarments and for emergencies).

■ Make sure that the caregiver knows of your loved one's allergies to medications, food, plants, etc.

■ Inform the caregiver what to do in case of an emergency. Provide him with a list of procedures to take if they are in a car accident or if you're loved one becomes ill, or suffers heart failure, for example, or gets lost. Review this information with him. Otherwise, he may tell you that you never told him what to do in certain situations. A caregiver cannot read your mind.

■ Make sure that you provide the caregiver with everything that she will need to know—physically and mentally—about your loved one.

■ Do not install "call waiting" on your loved one's telephone line. Doing so gives the caregiver free access to local phone calls all day without your knowledge.

Security Lock Box

Keep the key to the car and the petty cash in a security lock box. This way, the caregiver cannot claim that the key to the car was misplaced or that the money is not where it should be. The caregiver needs to leave the keys and the petty cash in the box after his shift is over. By having a locked box, you need not worry about your loved one gaining access to the car keys. The key for the lock box should be kept in a spot designated by you. Instruct all of the caregivers to return the key to that spot. If your loved one does not live with you, provide a check list for the caregiver to refer to everyday at the end of each shift.

Identification Card

If your loved one is no longer able to drive, make sure to take away his drivers license and get an identification card immediately. The Department of Motor Vehicles will provide you with the identification card. A person with dementia could get lost and may not be able to tell anyone his address, telephone number, or other emergency contact information.

Identification Bracelet

The Alzheimer's Association has reported that over 70 percent of Alzheimer's patients will wander. Get your loved one an identification bracelet or necklace. This way, if she gets lost, she can be identified immediately. The Alzheimer's Association can provide appropriate identification.

Photographs

Caregivers need several photos of your loved one to give to security in case of situations like this. You can also provide the caregiver with homemade, laminted photo identification cards which includes a picture of your loved one and the name, age, height, weight, address, and telephone number of your loved one.

Insurance

Check your homeowner's insurance policy or renter's insurance policy to make sure it covers household employees. If your caregiver gets hurt in your home while working for you, you could be liable for the injuries. This insurance should be in place before the caregiver starts working.

The Proper Equipment

■ HOSPITAL BED: Your loved one may need to have a special bed for their illness, rehabilitation, and proper support.

■ SPECIAL MATTRESS: If your loved one is confined to a bed, purchase a special mattress to avoid bedsores. Your loved one must be rotated every one to two hours to prevent bedsores, which are very difficult to avoid when a special mattress is not being used. Medical supply companies sell different kinds of mattresses that vibrate, inflate, and deflate.

■ HEAL GUARDS: You can purchase heal guards that will protect your loved one's heals from bedsores. Heal guards provide a cushion between the heal and bed.

■ MATTRESS PAD COVERS: Medical supply stores

sell mattress pad covers that are waterproof and can either be disposed of or washed.

■ CHANGING PADS: These pads are excellent to place in the bed and on sofas. If your incontinent loved one is sitting on them, the changing pads will ensure that the mattress and or furniture remain dry.

■ GRAB BARS: I cannot stress the importance of grab bars enough, especially in the bathrooms. Most elderly patients end up falling and breaking bones very easily. If the bars are available, the patient can grab the bars to prevent himself from slipping and falling.

■ COMMODE: A commode is a portable potty that can be placed next to your loved one's bed to prevent your loved one from tripping in the night while walking to the bathroom.

■ NIGHT LIGHTS: Bright night lights should be placed throughout the home. In case of an emergency, the night lights will give your loved one ample light to see in the dark and escape danger.

■ BATHING CHAIR: If bathing your loved one becomes difficult, buy a chair for the bathtub or shower stall for your loved one to sit on while the caregiver uses a hand-held shower sprayer for

My Experience
Why Is the Food Gone?

I could not understand it. The food kept disappearing. The caregiver said that she and Marilyn loved going to the park. Unfortunatley, they were going to a park that my list did not permit. Where were the fruit and vegetables going? The caregiver claimed that Marilyn had a huge appetite and that she was eating extra fruits and vegetables. I decided to follow the caregiver. Everyday she took Marilyn to the park. Why was she doing this? What was in the bag? I proceeded to follow her and discovered that she was taking bags of Marilyn's food to someone in the park.

washing. An inexpensive hose can be purchased at your local hardware store.

Food Menu

Provide a menu for the caregiver. You can even make one menu for the month and then reuse the same menu every month. You will then know exactly how much each monthly grocery bill will be. I had a very big problem with the caregivers stealing food. I learned that by providing a menu, I knew exactly what Marilyn would be eating and, when I came to visit, I knew what food items needed to be there.

Provide a menu for breakfast lunch, dinner, dessert and snacks. List menus for each meal and describe how you would like the food prepared.

Do not assume that everyone you hire prepares food the same way you do. I found that when I typed a menu with a description, it was easier for the caregiver to prepare the food properly to Marilyn's taste. One caregiver had been cooking rice with olive oil. The caregiver thought that I was crazy to insist that the rice should be made with butter. Marilyn could not express how awful the oily rice tasted because she had stopped speaking. She just refused to eat it.

If you provide a menu for the month, you can keep rotating the menu every month instead of creating a new one. Choose maybe four or five different types of breakfast and have the caregiver rotate the breakfast choices. You will find that you will know how much you are spending on food every month and if your loved one does not live with you, you can pop in and make sure that the caregiver is making the appropriate menu for the evening and serving it to your loved one.

Daily Journal

Purchase a journal so that the caregiver, you, your other caregivers, and the doctors can monitor your loved one's diet and activities. Make every caregiver responsible for filling out the activity logbook daily. Read the log book frequently to check up on the caregiver.

If you live close to your loved one, check the Daily Journal weekly. If you live out of state, have the caregiver send you the Daily Journal at least once every two weeks. You can even set up a Daily Journal for the caregiver to send to you by e-mail every day. Periodically check the Daily Journal on a day that the caregiver does not expect you to, to make sure the caregiver is entering the information daily. Otherwise, the caregiver may be reporting inaccurate information.

Medication Log Book

A Medication Log Book includes the date, time, caregiver's name, types of medication, dosages given to the patient, and any side effects. It is imperative in emergencies to list what medication was given to the patient and at what time and day. On the inside of the cover of the Medication Log Book, attach a typed sheet listing the medications and dosages to be given to the patient and at what times. Do not rely on the caregiver to remember what medication should be given and when. Keep the medication out of the reach of the patient. Your loved one may not remember taking his medication and take another dose, creating complications or an emergency situation.

Chapter 3
FINDING A CAREGIVER

Evaluate your loved one's situation with your doctor so you can hire the type of caregiver that best suits your needs. Does he need minimal care? Does she need a companion? In our case, when Marilyn first became sick, she would forget some things but not everything. She needed someone to supervise her yet be her companion to the movies and lunches. We needed someone who could carry on a conversation, someone who looked like a friend rather than a nurse. These caregivers usually work for a daily, weekly, or monthly rate.

You will also have to decide between day care and live-in care. Day caregivers usually work hourly. Their rate depends on their qualifications and experience. You should also make sure that this person does not have other commitments that will interfere with her performance. The caregiver that you hire should be available to substitute for your other shift worker occasionally for sick days and vacations. Make sure that you hire a caregiver certified in CPR.

Five Types of Caregivers

COMPANION: Someone who cooks, cleans, accompanies your loved one to the movies, and converses with your loved one as a friend. In short, a companion is a caregiver who can keep your loved one company.

CERTIFIED NURSING ASSISTANT (CNA): A state Certified Nursing Assistant prepares meals, feeds your loved one, walks with your loved one, regards vital signs, repositions your bedridden loved one to prevent bedsores, helps your loved one use the urinal or bedpan, changes any dressings, and notes your loved one's changing mental, physical, and emotional conditions.

HOME HEALTH AID: This caregiver helps with the toilet or bedpan, prepares meals, checks breathing and pulse rates, has stimulating conversations with the patient, and does the household chores (making the bed, doing the laundry, and cleaning the bathroom and kitchen).

LICENSED VOCATIONAL NURSE (LVN): A state registered nurse trained to work with the mentally and physically challenged (handicapped, convalescents, and elderly), the LVN works with doctors to determine medical care for a patient.

These caregivers change dressings, take temperature, give intravenous fluids, and take blood pressure and pulse rates. They administer prescribed medications, give injections and draw blood. An LVN may also perform general housekeeping and cooking duties.

REGISTERED NURSE (RN): Most RNs work in acute care situations, such as hospitals, nursing facilities, and emergency centers. A Registered Nurse can supervise the patient's care and administers necessary treatment. In addition to performing the same duties as a Licensed Vocational Nurse, a Registered Nurse monitors the patient, records changes and symptoms, conducts complete physical examinations, and assists the doctor in minor surgeries. They may also give direction to the family, the patients, and other nursing assistants that may be working in the home.

Agencies

Agencies that provide caregivers can be located in your local telephone yellow pages under "Caregivers" or "Nurses." Before you agree to work with an agency, ask to see a copy of the Department of Health Report for their agency.

Every agency should make this report available to you. If you cannot go to the agency, call the Department of Health for this agency and make sure the records are to your satisfaction.

An agency should provide the following information on any potential candidate:

■ LIABILITY INSURANCE: Proof of liability insurance should be presented to you showing that the agency has coverage for an employee should that employee steal or causes physical or psychological harm to your loved one.

■ DEPARTMENT OF MOTOR VEHICLE REPORTS: A current report will show whether the caregiver has a good driving record.

■ CRIMINAL INVESTIGATION REPORTS: For agencies, a background check consists of a telephone call

---

My Experience
No Kidding

Does the candidate have small children? I hired a caregiver who had four small children between the ages of one and five. She actually drove Marilyn to her home so she could watch her children. Once she brought her youngest child to Marilyn's home. This is not acceptable.

to the State License Commission to validate the caregiver's license. Make sure that the caregivers fingerprints are run through the FBI. If the agency does not provide a report, obtain one on your own. Companies provide this service for roughly $100.

■ REFERENCES: Each caregiver should provide a list of his past employers with phone numbers and the job description. Verify the references. I was given a reference for a caregiver and found out through caller identification that the reference had the same last name as the caregiver.

■ COPY OF THE CAREGIVER'S DRIVER'S LICENSE: Always keep a copy of the caregiver's driver's license, especially if he is going to be chauffeuring your loved one.

■ COPY OF THE CAREGIVER'S SOCIAL SECURITY CARD: Keep a copy of the caregiver's Social Security card to report to the Internal Revenue Service and state.

■ NURSING STATE NUMBER AND COPY OF CAREGIVER'S CURRENT CERTIFICATE: After you receive the copy of the certificate, call the State Health

Department to check whether the nurse has been suspended or is under investigation. Do not rely on the agency to do this for you.

Fees

If you hire a caregiver through an agency, you will pay higher rates than if you had hired that same individual on you own. Call several agencies in your area to determine the going rate.

Beware

Most agencies provide only independent contractors. In other words, the caregivers are not employees of that agency. Most agencies will allow you to interview a few caregivers. Unfortunately, in most cases, the first candidates are not necessarily the ones you want. They may be the

---

My Experience
Double Check

I checked on several caregivers only to discover that their licenses were under investigation for neglect or abuse. This information was never supplied to me by the agencies.

---

only ones available at that time. The agency will tell you that they are some of the best caregivers they have. They will also demand a finder's fee.

Do not believe everything you are told, For instance, some agencies will tell you that the caregiver they are sending has worked with dementia patients, and after a week you will discover that she has never worked with dementia patients.

If you do not like the caregiver that you hire, you are stuck with the caregiver until the agency finds a replacement. Some agencies only permit up to three replacements.

Make sure you read the contract carefully before signing. Some agencies will ask you to fill out a form when you want to interview them. You need to make sure that the agency is the right agency for you before you start filling out forms and giving out information.

Ethnicity

Some agencies work with caregivers from certain ethnic backgrounds. I worked with one agency that worked primarily with Hungarian caregivers. Another agency had predominately Hispanic caregivers. Yet another agency worked mainly with Asian caregivers. Never judge a person by their ethnicity. A bad experience with two caregivers from the same ethnic background does not mean that everyone with that ethnic background will be the same. Judge caregivers on a case-by-case basis, not by their race, religion, or creed.

Chapter 4
INTERVIEWING
AND HIRING
A CAREGIVER

Talk to the candidate on the telephone, briefly describe the position, and determine whether the candidate qualifies for the job. If you describe your loved one's condition accurately, the candidate will be able to tell you right away whether she is qualified for the job. If yes, schedule an interview and ask the candidate to bring a list of references (at least two or three) to the interview. Prepare a list of questions for the interview. Asking about the candidate's past work experiences is not enough. Ask the candidate to explain what he would do in a hypothetical situation.

Sample Interview Questions
- Tell me a little about yourself.
- Compliment the candidate on something and see how they respond.

- Do you have children?

- How long have you been a caregiver? Tell me about your past experiences with other clients. Where have you worked? Whom did you work for? What were your duties?

- How do you feel about caring for a person who is disabled or elderly?

- Have you ever worked for anyone who had a memory problem? Dementia? Parkinson's?

- Do you know what dementia is? (Or the illness afflicting your loved one). Tell me what you know about it.

- Have you ever had to cook for someone? What kind of meals did you prepare?

- Are you certified in CPR? If yes, may I see your certification? If no, would you be willing to become certified in CPR?
- Is your schedule flexible?
- What would you do if someone was very stubborn or became angry?
- The cable man is scheduled to arrive. The phone rings while you are giving Marilyn a bath. The cable man needs you to answer the phone and buzz him in the gate. What do you do?
- While dining in a restaurant, Marilyn takes off her bracelet. What do you do?
- What would you do if you are involved in a car accident?
- What would you do if Marilyn starts walking up to people in public and starts talking to them?

Interview

If possible, have your loved one present during the interview. The caregiver will be with your loved one on a day-to-day basis, so they need to feel comfortable with each another—even if your loved one has dementia or another illness. While you may consider a candidate exceptional, your loved one may not share that same feeling.

Write down a precise description of your loved one's condition, so the caregiver will understand the situation she will be facing. For example:

> "Marilyn appears to be 'normal.' What seems to be Marilyn's stubborn behavior is actually the result of Frontal Lobe Dementia.
>
> "Marilyn does not have Alzheimer's disease, although her short-term memory is faulty. You may have to repeat things several times.
>
> "When Marilyn says she needs to use the restroom, you must locate one immediately. If you are at the mall, she will probably wander away from you."

You need to tell the caregiver everything possible about your loved one to avoid any possible misunderstandings about her condition.

After the Interview

Immediately after the interview, write down what you liked and disliked about the candidate. If you and another family member are conducting interviews together, immediately discuss what each of you thought about the candidate.

My Experience
The Bathtub Quiz

When Marilyn was having trouble getting out of the bathtub, I asked several caregivers what they would do if Marilyn refused to get out of the tub. They all assured me that they were highly trained with dementia patients. I thought I was going to have difficulty choosing a caregiver—until I heard their answers:

- "I would offer a cookie."
- "I would knock on the wall and tell her to get out because someone was at the front door."
- "I would punch her in the arm. Then she would get up."

Unfortunately, none of these are the correct answer. The correct response is:

"I would gently guide the patient out of the bathtub by instructing her on every move. I would say, 'Marilyn, first slowly lift your left leg.' I would let her know that I am going to place my hand on her leg before I instruct her what to do next. I would gently help her glide her leg into the proper position."

Some caregivers will lie to get a job. Some caregivers will say anything to get the job.

The list can go on and on.

Do I Have a
Great Caregiver for You!

If a friend refers you to a caregiver, do not neglect to conduct a thorough background check, ask for letters of recommendation, and call the state to check the license. A friend of mine recommended her sister as a caregiver, claiming she had a lot of experience dealing with the elderly. I was delighted. A referral! Could it be this easy?

I met the woman and loved her. She was sweet, eloquent, said she had worked with people with dementia, and, when I gave her the scenario test, she passed with excellence. I was so relieved to find a caregiver; I hired her without checking her background.

Two days before she was going to start, I had second thoughts. I decided to conduct a quick background check, certain everything would be fine. To my surprise, I learned this woman had just been released from prison. She had served several years in prison for selling drugs. My friend, knowing her sister was desperate for a job, referred her to me without telling me the full story.

If you need a caregiver, ask friends, coworkers, neighbors, and friends for referrals—but always conduct a background check.

Hire at Least Two Caregivers

If your loved one needs full-time care, hire at least two caregivers to work alternative shifts. This way, if one caregiver gets sick or wants to take a vacation, you can ask the other caregiver to cover her shift. Have the second caregiver come in for a few hours to observe the way the first caregiver handles the situation, to better understand the procedures you require. If you fail to hire a second caregiver, when your caregiver gets ill and you cannot take care of your loved one yourself, you will be forced to call an agency. You will get deeply involved with the daily care of your loved one; impeding your ability to interview another candidate.

If you can only hire one caregiver, do not let that caregiver work more than five days a week with your loved one. A good caregiver needs a break. Otherwise, he will begin to lose patience. If you depend on only one caregiver, she may become demanding, realizing that you rely solely on her. Remember, even if you think you have the best caregiver, anyone can be replaced.

Before you hire the caregiver, obtain a copy of the caregiver's:

- Driver's license
- Driving record (The caregiver can obtain this from the Department of Motor Vehicles.)
- Nursing license/certificate (Make sure the dates are valid. Then call the local licensing number and find out if there are any complaints or pending cases against this caregiver.)
- Social security card

Chapter 5
JOB DESCRIPTION

Prepare a thorough job description for your caregiver to delineate your expectations. This will help prevent any possible misunderstandings. Keep a copy of the job description posted in the house at all times where the caregiver is working.

Sit down with the caregiver and read aloud every section of the job description to the caregiver and after each section asks if he understands what you have read, then have the caregiver sign the job description. Do not trust the caregiver to read the job description on his own. You want to make certain that all your rules and expectations are clearly understood.

Keep the signed original and give the caregiver a copy. This way the caregiver can review the job description at any time.

CAREGIVER JOB DESCRIPTION

I understand my Job Description as specified below and what is required from me. I understand that if I ever have any questions, I can call Carrie or Jay Bruder at any time. I understand that if Marilyn is ever injured or hurt in any way that I must contact Carrie or Jay immediately. Carrie's home number is (555) 555-5555 and her cellular phone number is (555) 555-5555. Jay's cellular phone number is (555) 555-5555 and his work number is (555)555-5555.

_____   _____
Signature   Date

Printed Name _____
Address _____
Phone _____
Social Security Number _____
Days _____
Hours _____

I. General Job Description

A. The Caregiver is responsible for the care of Marilyn during the hours specified above.

B. All behavior toward Marilyn must be respectful, and conversations with Marilyn are to be courteous and kept in a low-tone to maintain calmness. Kindness and patience are expected at all times. Caregiver will not raise her voice, use abusive language, nor use force with Marilyn at any time.

C. The caregiver shall contact Carrie Bruder immediately by phone or cellular phone should any emergency or uncontrollable situation arise.

D. If Marilyn is in need of medical attention, caregiver will call 911 immediately and then notify Carrie Bruder.

E. If Marilyn becomes ill, falls, or is injured in any way, the caregiver shall inform Carrie Bruder immediately. If the caregiver notices any bruises on Marilyn during her shift, the caregiver shall inform Carrie Bruder immediately.

F. The Caregiver shall execute any direction received from either Carrie or Jay Bruder pertaining to the care of Marilyn. If the caregiver is unable to perform any duties required, care-

My Experience
Common Sense

A caregiver named Sue received a phone call from an unknown telemarketer. She gave this unsolicited caller my name, phone number, and address. This company would not stop harassing me. Sue insisted that she didn't know she wasn't supposed to give out information. Another caregiver gave out Marilyn's credit card number over the phone and we received a cooking product in the mail that we could not return.

giver shall immediately notify Carrie Bruder and give the reason why the caregiver is unable to carry out the direction.

G. If the caregiver is for any reason unable to work a scheduled shift, the caregiver must give Carrie Bruder 24-hour notice. If the caregiver is going to arrive late to work on any specific day, the caregiver is to contact Carrie prior to the caregiver's usual check in time. Continued absenteeism or tardiness may be grounds for termination of employment.

II. Hygiene

The caregiver shall maintain Marilyn's good hygiene as follows:

A. Bathing and shampooing: The caregiver will bathe and shampoo Marilyn accordingly:

1. Before bathing Marilyn, the caregiver shall bring a fresh diaper and towel into the bathroom.

2. The caregiver and only the caregiver shall turn on the water and monitor the water temperature.

3. During the bath, the caregiver shall never leave Marilyn alone in the bathroom.

4. The caregiver shall place Marilyn in the chair in the bathtub and wash her accordingly.

5. After drying Marilyn with a towel, the caregiver shall remove the bottle of moisturizer lotion from the bottom cabinet and apply the lotion to Marilyn's body.

My Experience

Dinner at Eight

I had hired a new caregiver named Betty. I decided to go to Marilyn's house to make sure that Betty was adhering to the menu. I walked in at 7:40 P.M. to find that Betty had just finished eating dinner and she was enjoying ice cream for dessert. Marilyn had not yet eaten. Betty explained that she wanted to eat first because Marilyn took too long to eat. This meant that Marilyn would not be eating until at least eight o'clock at night.

B. Feeding: The caregiver will assist with feeding Marilyn.

C. Brushing and styling hair

D. Toileting (including changing adult diapers if needed)

E. Dressing: Make sure that your caregiver has a routine when dressing your loved one.

F. Applying makeup for patient: Only if needed. Do not allow caregiver to apply eye makeup.

G. Maintaining good skin care: Be sure to buy plenty of lotion and or special cream for diaper rash.

H. Shaving: Be sure to buy razors that will not cut your loved one.

I. Brushing teeth: Caregiver shall use the provided electric toothbrush to brush Marilyn's teeth twice a day. (If your loved one will not allow you to use a tooth brush, get a wash cloth and gently have the caregiver clean your loved one's teeth.)

III. Housekeeping

The caregiver shall perform the following house-keeping duties:

A. Laundry:
1. The caregiver shall wash Marilyn's dirty laundry, sheets, pillow cases, and towels.
2. The caregiver shall launder Marilyn's clothes in cold water, dry the clothes in the dryer, fold the clothes and return them to her room in the appropriate locations (closet or dresser drawers). Any dirty clothing with a tag marked "dry clean only" shall be given to Carrie every Friday.
3. The caregiver shall check Marilyn's sheets daily to determine if they are soiled. If the sheets are soiled, the caregiver shall launder them immediately, and remake the bed with clean sheets.
4. The caregiver shall launder Marilyn's sheets every Wednesday and launder the bathroom rugs every Sunday.

B. Food preparation: Specify the schedule for meals and snacks. Instruct the caregiver what to prepare and how to prepare the meal, if necessary. Let the caregiver know how many snacks a day should be given to your loved one.

C. Vacuuming: If you would like the caregiver to

vacuum the house, let her know exactly how often you would like the carpets vacuumed.

D. Cleaning the house (including mopping and dusting). Let the caregiver know how often this task should be done. Insist that the bathrooms be kept spotless.

E. Washing dishes: The caregiver shall wash the dishes, rinse food out of the kitchen sink, keep counters and floor clean at all times, and mop and hand-dry the floor when needed.

F. Dishwasher: When the dishwasher is full, the caregiver shall add detergent and start the machine. When the cycle ends, the caregiver shall empty the dishwasher properly. If the caregiver arrives on duty and the dishes are clean in the dishwasher, the caregiver shall empty it.

G. Living Room: The caregiver shall keep entry floors clean and the coffee table neat at all times. Drinking glasses shall not be placed directly on the table. Instead, drinking glasses shall be placed on top of the coasters provided in the top

My Experience
Out of Control

The caregiver felt that Marilyn was fully capable of using the remote control to close the garage door because she let her close it before without any problems—until Marilyn closed the garage door onto the roof of the car.

drawer of the coffee table. No shoes are permitted on the sofa or the coffee table.

H. Newspaper: The caregiver shall place all the used newspapers in the recycling bin every Sunday evening.

I. Lock Up: The caregiver shall turn off the lights in the laundry room and garage at the end of each shift. The caregiver shall be responsible for locking and bolting the front door and the garage door at all times.

J. Curtains: The caregiver shall draw the curtains at sunset.

K. Failure to perform any of these duties may be grounds for immediate termination.

L. The caregiver shall not use or be in possession of drugs or alcohol, possess firearms, or be involved in any other illegal behavior.

M. The caregiver shall not smoke while at work at any time.

N. The caregiver shall report to Carrie Bruder upon checking in to work and must check out with Carrie or Jay Bruder at the end of the shift.

O. Garbage: The caregiver shall remove the trash at the end of each shift.

P. House Plants: The caregiver shall water the houseplants during the day shift.

Q. Visitors: A day caregiver is not permitted to have visitors. A live-in caregiver may have visitors if and only if the visit is approved first by Carrie or Jay. At no time shall the caregiver have overnight guest.

R. Mail: The caregiver shall not receive mail, packages, or deliveries without clearance from Carrie or Jay.

S. Animals: The caregiver shall not bring any animals or pets to or into Marilyn's house at any time.

T. Off-Limits: The caregiver may not enter the storage closet or the home office at any time.

U. Theft: Stealing of any kind shall not be tolerated and is grounds for immediate termination.

IV. Daily Journal

A. The caregiver shall maintain a Daily Journal to record Marilyn's activities for the day including:

1. Who checked in with you when you arrived?
2. How was Marilyn when you arrived and what was she doing?
3. What meals did you prepare and how much did Marilyn eat and drink during your time with her?
4. List all bowel movements, constipation, etc.
5. Specify every location to which you and Marilyn traveled throughout the day.
6. Who called and who visited?

B. The caregiver shall make all journal entries on the same day worked. Carrie may come by and pick up the journal to review at any time.

C. All receipts must be taped to the adjacent left hand page of the Daily Journal. If an establishment does not provide a receipt, the caregiver shall obtain a receipt from the manager. If the receipt does not indicate the name of the establishment, the caregiver shall write the name of the business at the top of the receipt and initial it.

D. Daily Journal entries shall be recorded in the style of the sample on the following pages.

V. Medication

A. The caregiver shall administer daily medications in the proper doses as provided.

B. The caregiver shall list all medication administered to Marilyn in the Medication Journal, specifying the time the dosage is given.

C. Depending on qualifications a caregiver may: monitor treatment, take pulse, change dressing, take blood pressure, give injections, monitor diet and physical activity, assess mental

DAILY JOURNAL ENTRIES

Car Odometer
   Beginning Reading: <u>135,000</u> miles
   Final Reading: <u>135,020 miles</u>

Petty Cash
   Beginning Balance $<u>50.00</u>
   Ending Balance $<u>25.30</u>

10:00 A.M.
   Phoned Carrie to check-in. Marilyn was in a
      happy mood.

10:00-10:15 A.M.
   Breakfast: Two waffles with jelly, melon and
      8 oz glass of Orange Juice

10:15 A.M.
   Bowel movement.

10:30-11:00 A.M.
   Gave Marilyn a bath and dressed her for the
      day.

11:00 A.M. - 1:00 P.M.
   Went out to the Edwards Cinema in the
      Commons for a movie. Marilyn ate a small
      popcorn and had a small juice. We saw the
      movie <u>Shrek</u>. Marilyn enjoyed the movie.

1:30-2:30 P.M.

Lunch at Baja Fresh. Marilyn ate half of her chicken burrito and drank half of her lemonade. (cost $10.45)

3:00-3:30 P.M.

We went to Baskin Robbins for ice cream. Marilyn ate a small cone of chocolate ice cream. (cost $5.95)

4:00-5:00 P.M.

Doctor appointment with Dr. Bruce Miller. Marilyn used the restroom (urine only) and drank two bottles of water.

5:30-6:30 P.M.

Prepared dinner. Roasted Chicken, Green Beans & Rice. Marilyn ate 3/4 of Chicken, approximately 8 of the green beans and all of her rice from the rice bowl. Drank one large glass of milk.

7:00-8:30 P.M.

Watched _Wheel of Fortune_ and played a game of checkers with Marilyn.

9:00 P.M.

Prepared Marilyn for bed. She had a toothache, so I called Carrie immediately.

and physical conditions, conduct physical examinations, keep medical charts, draw blood, take temperature, and more.

D. The caregiver shall maintain a Medication Journal, listing all medications and dosages given to Marilyn and at what times.

VI. Companionship

A. Reading: You may want to have the caregiver read to your loved one if she can no longer read on her own.

B. Walking/exercise: If your loved one is able to exercise, make sure that the caregiver puts him on a daily routine of walking or exercising.

C. Conversation: It is very important for the caregiver to always carry on a conversation with your loved one. The stimulation is very good for her brain.

D. Movies/Plays: You may want your loved one to see movies or plays with your caregiver.

E. Music: Perhaps while the caregiver prepares meals, your loved one can listen to the music that she enjoys.

F. Artwork: It is very stimulating for the brain to create artwork. You could buy some paper and even crayons to give your loved one something to do if he is not mobile.

VII. Expenditures

A. Credit Card: Marilyn shall be issued a credit card to be used only with permission by Carrie or Jay. The caregiver must make every effort to contact Carrie or Jay for verbal approval prior to any purchase. The credit card is to be kept in Marilyn's wallet. Marilyn is the only individual authorized to sign for a purchase. All credit card receipts must contain the date, place, and time and shall be initialed by the caregiver. All credit card receipts are to be given to Carrie. All unauthorized and unaccountable purchases shall be charged back to the caregiver. The caregiver is not permitted to take the credit card during off-hours for any reason. No alcoholic beverages may be purchased.

B. Petty Cash: All cash expenses for recreation (movies, ice cream) are to be purchased from petty cash. Petty cash will be replenished weekly upon accounting of all approved purchase receipts. Improper use of petty cash and/or improper maintenance of cash receipts may be grounds for termination of employment. All cash receipts must include the date, place, time, and must be initialed by the caregiver. The caregiver shall tape the receipts in the journal on the date they were issued. Petty cash may not be used to purchase alcoholic beverages.

C. Gifts: The caregiver shall not be permitted to accept any items or money from Marilyn as a "gift" or a "loan." Under no circumstances and at no time shall the caregiver present Marilyn with a gift of any kind. The caregiver shall not borrow or wear any of Marilyn's possessions at any time.

> *My Experience*
> ## Phony Excuses
>
> I discovered a caregiver talking on the phone for over an hour while Marilyn was watching television. If your caregiver has nothing to do but talk on the phone, assign more duties or schedule more activities such as playing cards, board games, or arts and crafts. You are not paying the caregiver to come over and chat on the phone, neglecting your loved one.

D. General Shopping: The caregiver is authorized to purchase lunch and snack food and pay any parking fees (excluding valet parking). Hair care and waxing are permitted for Marilyn only. Carrie will set appointments. Painting ceramics is to be done by Marilyn and supervised by the caregiver.

VIII. Meals

A. Carrie must approve acceptable restaurants before the caregiver takes Marilyn to lunch. The caregiver shall prepare breakfast and dinner for Marilyn at home unless Carrie instructs the caregiver to bring Marilyn to another location for breakfast or dinner.

B. For meals prepared at home, Marilyn has difficulty with large portions. Only small portions are to be served on the plate. Marilyn is to be

I hired a caregiver named Nancy right before the holidays. She was dressed in very nice slacks and a sweater. A week later, Nancy brought Marilyn to our home to celebrate the holidays. We were having twenty-five guests. To my surprise, Nancy came to the door wearing a hot pink mini-skirt, a low-cut blouse, and five-inch high heels. I did not even recognize her because she wore so much makeup. The minute she sat down, we could see her underwear. Embarrassed by her inappropriate attire, I felt compelled to have a chat with Nancy.

Clearly inform the caregiver what is acceptable dress. Some families prefer to have the caregiver in a white uniform and nursing shoes. Since Marilyn was still going out frequently, we wanted the caregivers to dress casually yet tastefully.

given her plate at the table with a table cloth (or place mat) and a napkin. If she does not finish the meal at the table, Marilyn can eat with a tray at the coffee table. If Marilyn is having a hard time eating, the caregiver shall feed her. Marilyn is to eat her dinner before the caregiver does. After she is completely finished with her meal, the caregiver may eat her meal.

C. Marilyn will pay for scheduled meals out. No one other than the caregiver may accompany

Marilyn to a restaurant, nor shall Marilyn pay for anyone's meals or beverages other than for herself and the caregiver, unless authorized by Carrie or Jay. If the caregiver is working a full day, meals will be provided for that day. If the caregiver is working night care only, meals will not be provided.

D. All lunch expenditures when dining out should not exceed $25 (if the cost does exceed this amount, an explanation may be required). The caregiver must buy and eat lunch at lunchtime. The caregiver is not permitted to buy lunch to take home.

E. Dehydration: Since Marilyn is unable to ask for water on her own, the caregiver will monitor Marilyn's fluid intake to prevent dehydration. The caregiver will give Marilyn at least eight glasses of water per day in addition to other fluids. The caregiver shall monitor the water intake in the Daily Journal to help keep track.

IX. Automobile

A. The caregiver is permitted to drive Marilyn's car only to take Marilyn out. The car may be driven only within the West Valley area—unless specific direction has been pre-approved by Carrie. Neither Marilyn nor any other person is permitted to drive the vehicle at any time (with the exception of Jay or Carrie). The caregiver may not drive anyone in Marilyn's car except Marilyn. The caregiver may not drive Marilyn's car unless accompanied by Marilyn. The caregiver shall record the mileage reading on the vehicle odometer into the Daily Journal before using the vehicle and the mileage upon finishing use of the vehicle on that same day. When the car is not in use, the caregiver shall keep the car parked in Marilyn's garage.

B. When the car is parked, the caregiver shall store the car keys in the security lock box.

C. There shall be no eating or drinking in the car. If the caregiver brings a doggie bag home from a restaurant, it should be placed on the floor in the back seat of the car.

D. The caregiver is responsible for locking the car at all times and for removing the CD player from the dashboard and locking it in the glove compartment when the vehicle is not in use.

X. Telephone

A. The caregiver is not permitted to make personal phone calls on Marilyn's telephone. Only Marilyn may use the telephone unless the caregiver is contacting Jay or Carrie. The caregiver is not permitted to use a cellular phone at work, except in the case of an emergency situation. The caregiver may make collect calls in emergency situations.

XI. Dress Code

A. The caregiver shall not wear heals that are over two inches, extremely short skirts or dresses, low-cut blouses, or sweat clothes.
B. Pants are acceptable.
C. Long hair must be tied back when preparing food for Marilyn.

XII. General Rules

A. Visitors: A day caregiver is not permitted to have visitors. A live-in caregiver may have visitors if the visit is first approved by Carrie or Jay. At no time shall the caregiver have an overnight guest in Marilyn's house.
B. The caregiver shall never leave Marilyn alone when out of the home.
C. When away from the house, the caregiver shall hold Marilyn's arm at all times.
D. The caregiver shall not give out any information to anyone regarding Marilyn or her family.
E. The caregiver shall not give Carrie or Jay's tele-

phone number to anyone. If someone needs to talk to Carrie or Jay or wants information regarding Marilyn, the caregiver shall pass along the information to Carrie or Jay.

Schedule
(Times are approximate)

8:30 A.M.: Awaken Marilyn. Get her out of bed gently and talk about what activities are planned for the day. Change her adult diaper and prepare her for bathing. After she has been bathed, apply lotion to her skin, blow-dry her hair, brush her teeth, dress her in fresh clean clothes and jewelry, and gently guide her to the living room. Make sure that Marilyn has her eyeglasses with her at all times.

9:30 A.M.: Serve Marilyn breakfast.

11:00 A.M.: Serve Marilyn a snack.

12:30 A.M.: Serve Marilyn lunch.

3:00 P.M.: Serve Marilyn a snack.

6:00 P.M.: Serve Marilyn dinner.

7:00 P.M.: Serve Marilyn dessert.

10:00 P.M.: Bedtime. Help Marilyn brush her teeth and wash her face. Place Marilyn in bed, remove her eyeglasses, and place them next to her on her nightstand.

Chapter 6
PHYSICAL CHANGES

Provide the caregiver with a written description of your loved ones physical changes at each phase of her illness. This will better familiarize the caregiver with your loved one's present condition. For example:

Marilyn's Physical Changes

■ Due to her slow motor skills, Marilyn cannot be rushed or hurried to perform any task, routine, or activity. When rushed she becomes anxious, confused, and un-cooperative. Marilyn's memory capacity has decreased to the point where, though she is somewhat aware of what is happening around her, she cannot remember her daily activities and gets everything confused. She sometimes behaves as if she is lost or withdrawn. For instance, if you ask her what she ate for lunch or what she did during the day, she will answer the first thing that comes to her mind (which is usually incorrect).

■ Marilyn speaks according to what is being said around her. Her only form of communication is to repeat what she hears said by other people, on television, or on the radio. She does not repeat complete sentences, only the words that interest her, which she repeats continuously, not knowing when to stop. When this happens, she gets a strained look on her face. Attracting her attention makes her stop.

■ Marilyn tends to pick up inedible objects and attempts to eat them. For instance, if you give her a wrapped granola bar, she will eat the bar and the wrapper, without any qualms. She will also eat banana and orange peels.

■ Marilyn has lost the ability to display appropriate table manners and etiquette. If she is not watched closely at these times, she may behave strangely. For example, she may wipe her mouth excessively with a napkin causing her lips to get raw and bleed. The solution is to give her a napkin when it is time to wipe her mouth and then gently take it away from her. If there is no napkin, she will wipe her mouth with the back of her hand and then wipe her hand on her clothes.

■ Marilyn has recently developed the unconscious habit of pulling up her skirt to rub her knees in public. It has become necessary to dress Marilyn in pants before bringing her out in public for her dignity and safety.

■ Marilyn needs assistance with everything she does. The caregivers must brush her hair, feed her, dress her, and monitor and perform all of her personal hygiene. At meals, Marilyn must constantly be told to eat, how much food to put on her fork, to lift up the fork, and to put the food into her mouth. When she does finally perform a simple task, she does so by continually repeating what she has been instructed to do.

■ Marilyn does not seem to know when her appetite has been satisfied or when to stop eating. She does better at eating finger foods because she does not have to think about how to use utensils. The caregiver needs to monitor her meals so that all meals are balanced properly.

If you do not live with your loved one, make sure that you frequently check to see how your loved one is doing. If you live out of town and cannot see your loved one, have a friend periodically check on your loved one. If you rely on your caregivers to take your loved one to the doctor, make sure that the doctor calls you with the prognosis. Do not get the prognosis from your caregiver.

Chapter 7
DRIVING

If you are going to let the caregiver drive your car, purchase an umbrella car insurance policy. The cost averages approximately $250 per year, depending on the city in which you live.

Never let the caregiver use her car to chauffeur your loved one unless you have full insurance coverage and an umbrella policy. Otherwise, if the caregiver gets into an accident while working for you, you will be liable for any damages. Do not rely on the caregiver to provide this kind of additional insurance.

Give the caregiver a driving test before you allow her to drive your vehicle and chauffeur your loved one. Review all of the operating instructions for your vehicle with the caregiver. Do not permit the caregiver to chauffeur anyone but your loved one in the car.

> *My Experience*
> ## "Oh, I Thought You Said We Could Visit Friends"
>
> One caregiver thought I had given her permission to bring Marilyn to visit with the caregiver's friends. The caregiver interpreted "visiting friends" as visiting her friends. I meant that Marilyn could visit Marilyn's friends. Deep down, I knew the caregiver intentionally exceeded my rules, but I did fail to make myself perfectly clear. Clarify your rules so your loved one doesn't get stuck visiting someone with whom she has no interest spending time.

SHOPPING: If you allow the caregiver to take your loved one shopping, specify exactly which malls, stores, and markets are acceptable and which ones are off limits. This includes how far and to what areas she is allowed to drive your loved one.

DINING OUT: Provide a typed list of the permissible restaurants.

DELIVERING MAIL TO POST OFFICE: If the caregiver delivers mail to the post office, make sure it is only for your loved one.

VISITING FRIENDS: Make certain that the caregiver has directions to all relatives and friends your loved one will be visiting. Inform the caregiver that she is not allowed to take your loved one to the caregiver's friends' homes.

DOCTOR AND DENTAL APPOINTMENTS: If you want the caregiver to take your loved one to doctor appointments, give the caregiver a list of medications with the dosages for each. Instruct the caregiver to provide each doctor with a list of these medications, especially before any other medication is administered or prescribed. Send a written letter to the doctor stating that you—not the caregiver—will make all evaluations and decisions and that you should be called after the visit with the prognosis. Do not rely on the caregiver to tell you what the doctor has said.

My Experience
A Hair-Raising Story

Marilyn had an appointment at a hairdressing salon. Her caregiver decided to go out and buy something to eat while Marilyn was getting her hair done. When the hairdresser walked away, so did Marilyn. She walked right out the door. Fortunately, the caregiver returned just in time to find Marilyn wandering in the mall.

PICKING UP MEDICATIONS: If you are having the caregiver pick up the medications from a pharmacy, instruct him to check the label on the bottle against the list of medications that you have provided.

DRIVING TO HAIR SALON OR BARBERSHOP: Make prior arrangements with the hair salon or parlor so that the hairdresser is aware of the situation. Instruct the caregiver to stay with your loved one at all times. The hairdresser is not the babysitter and cannot be responsible for your loved one.

Chapter 8
PAYING A CAREGIVER

Depending on the state in which you live, you may be required to pay federal and state taxes. Contact the Internal Revenue Service at (800)-TAX-FORM and request Publication 926 which outlines everything you need to know about Household employees. You can also download publications and forms from www.irs.gov. Listed below are the other forms you will be required to fill out and return to the IRS:

- W-2 (issued by employers and stating how much an employee was paid in a year)
- W-3 (a transmittal form sent to the Social Security Administration)
- W-4 (A form completed by an employee to indicate his exemptions and status)
- 940 (used to report your annual Federal Unemployment Tax Act tax)

- 942 (for quarterly taxes)
- 1099 (for temporary employees)

Depending on the state in which you live, you may be required to pay state taxes (including quarterly state withholding), unemployment, and disability. You may also be required to fill out a verification of employment form for your state. This should be kept with you at all times.

If you fail to pay taxes for your household employees, you could be forced to pay penalties and interest. Many states offer free classes to explain everything you need to know about filling out the Internal Revenue Service forms and the state forms. However, if you need assistance and cannot handle this task, a variety of organizations will assist you, especially if you are a senior. You may also wish to use a computer tax program, like TurboTax or TaxAct. Or you may prefer to hire a payroll service to complete all of the necessary federal and state tax forms for you for a fee.

Checking In and Out

It is vital that the caregiver checks in and out with you before and after their shift. If you live out of town, you may consider getting a time clock so that the caregiver can punch in and out and be accounted for. This keeps the caregivers punctual. If you do not check them in and out, they will take advantage of the situation and cease being punctual.

Time Sheets

Create a time sheet for every caregiver to record the time the caregiver arrives and the time she departs. Caregivers have told me that they lost their time sheet or forgot to fill it out and could not remember the hours they worked. One caregiver called in sick but then claimed he had worked for me that day. Every caregiver fills in his own time sheet and signs it. By keeping a daily log to record when each caregiver checks in and out, you will be letting the caregiver know that you keep records. Tell them that they will not be on the clock until they checked in. This prevents the caregivers from lying.

Payment

Instruct the caregiver to fill out a biweekly time sheet and turn it into you on the first day of the month and the fifteenth day of each month.

Pay the caregiver with a paycheck on the second of the month and the sixteenth of the month. (If you prefer, pay the caregiver weekly or monthly, depending upon your arrangement with the caregiver).

Chapter 9
WHEN TO FIRE
A CAREGIVER

Most caregivers last an average of eight to ten months. A good caregiver lasts more than a year. If you have any doubt about a caregiver, listen to your instincts and find someone else. You may not wish to endure the hassle to find someone else, and you may not think you can find someone as good, but you can. You are the boss.

When a caregiver starts telling you what to do and what he is going to do, you need to let him go. When you instruct him how to do something and he objects, he needs to go.

Most caregivers try to take on more working hours than they can handle. Caring for sick individuals who require a lot of attention is like working with small children. The caregiver needs a lot of patience and frequent breaks. Most caregivers do not get the typical "lunch break." They are with your loved one for forty hours a week, which can be overwhelming and exhausting.

The Alzheimer's Association reports that 80 percent of Alzheimer caregivers suffer from stress and half of those caregivers also suffer from depression. Be able to recognize the signs of Caregiver Burnout before you hire a caregiver or before you take on the role of caregiver yourself.

Five Common Signs of Caregiver Burnout
1. Even though the caregiver is extremely depressed or stressed, he will deny both.

My Experience

The Caregiver Has Become My Boss

I hired a caregiver who seemed amazing, compliant, and willing to learn. For the first six months everything went smoothly. Then I invited her to my home for dinner with our family. After that, she felt comfortable with our family and when I told her what to do, she would do the opposite and tell me she felt her way was better. I would instruct her to take Marilyn to a play, and she would say she did not feel like going. This is not acceptable. Once a caregiver starts to turn the tables and tell you what to do, *fire her*.

2. The caregiver will be irritable, moody, negative, anxious, and showing signs of exhaustion.

3. The caregiver may start getting angry.

4. The caregiver may have a problem sleeping, show signs of health problems, or display a lack of concentration.

5. The caregiver may withdraw socially.

If you observe these changes in your caregiver, do not wait until it is too late. Too many elderly patients are abused everyday. Do not allow your loved one to become a statistic.

Common Signs of Abuse

Injuries and marks, which cannot be explained by the patient's medical condition or illness, can be signs of abuse. Check the location, the shape, and the repetition of the injury. Ask your loved one what happened and, if they are able to explain coherently, *listen!* Take note of:

■ Unexplained bruises or welts in patterns and in various stages of discoloration

■ Bedsores and poor skin hygiene (indicates neglect, which is considered abuse)

■ Scratches, cuts, pinch marks, bruises, lacerations or puncture wounds

■ Any injury that looks like it may have been caused by a belt, electric cords, or any other unusual object

■ Malnourishment or malnutrition

■ Bloody underclothing or torn clothing

■ Bleeding, swelling, or bruises in the external genitalia, vaginal, or anal areas

■ Unusual objects found in the vagina or rectum

■ Oddly shaped burns, which may be caused by cigarettes, chains, ropes, scalding water, clothes irons, or radiators

■ Name-calling, yelling, swearing, belittling,

frightening, threatening, or intimidation (all of which constitute verbal abuse)

■ Lack of access to food, shelter, or a bathroom

■ Facial injuries as minor as pinch marks or as major as black eyes, a broken nose, broken jaw, or swollen or bloody lips

■ Fractures or broken bones

■ Any suggestions/statements from your loved one that sexual abuse activity is occurring

■ Statements by your loved one that he has been beaten, locked up, or left without supervision

If you suspect any of this abuse or neglect, telephone Social Services and the police. There is a special hot line for elderly abuse in Califor-

My Experience
The Nightmare

A caregiver who had been caring for Marilyn for a few years telephoned to tell me that Marilyn had turned on the hot water while in the bathtub, the skin on her legs had turned a little red, but she was fine. The next morning, the caregiver telephoned to check in and asked me if she could buy some Neosporin for Marilyn's "tiny blister." I instructed her to bring Marilyn to my home so I could see the blister and so Marilyn could eat breakfast with her grandchildren.

An hour passed. When the caregiver and Marilyn finally pulled up to our house, I walked outside to greet them and discovered that the caregiver had dressed Marilyn in long pants and knee socks.

I pulled down Marilyn's socks to discover that the caregiver had wrapped her second and third degree burns with gauze. I lifted the gauze and became sick to my stomach.

I ran into the house to get ice. The caregiver insisted that the burns did not look bad. Marilyn could not express her pain to me, but I could see it on her face.

As I drove Marilyn to the burn center, she was shaking badly and vomiting. All I could do was cry. I felt horrible, convinced I had failed her. The doctor worked for over an hour to remove the gauze. Marilyn required surgery three different times, including skin graphs. I stayed with her until the night and every day after that. She would still smile at me. This poor woman had been abused and neglected, and her caregiver showed up at the hospital acting as if she had done nothing wrong.

"Too bad that Marilyn burned herself," she said.

The doctor asked her, "Couldn't you see how bad this was? Why didn't you tell her family?"

The caregiver replied, "It didn't look that bad to me." She never apologized.

I fired the caregiver, called the police, and had her investigated. Most importantly, I wrote several letters to Social Services and followed up with daily phone calls until I received written confirmation that her license was officially revoked. When I received that letter, I felt relieved that this caregiver would never be allowed to injure another patient again.

I had hired a company to install video cameras in Marilyn's home to monitor the caregiver. Unfortunately, the company was scheduled to install the cameras the day after Marilyn was burned.

A few weeks later, the caregiver had the audacity to call to demand that I send a letter of recommendation to her, otherwise she threatened to do something bad to me. I never sent the letter. Instead, I called the police. I refused to let this irresponsible person traumatize another family.

nia. Other states have abuse hot line numbers as well. Do not take these matters into your own hands. Make sure that the authorities are advised and investigating everything.

Listen to your inner voice. If your gut instinct tells you something is wrong, take appropriate action immediately.

Chapter 10
NURSING HOMES

Assisted Living

An Assisted Living Facility is a place where your loved one can live freely and still have assistance with daily living. It is like living in a community of friends. Assisted Living Facilities provide activities, meals, and basic assistance with everyday living. Your loved one who is still in his right mind could feel like he still lives on his own with the freedom to participate in daily activities with other seniors. You have the assurance that your loved one is not alone in her home, is actually with other people, and still gets the privacy and respect that he needs.

If you live far from your loved one, you may encounter difficulty finding a nursing home on your own. You can hire a service to find a nursing home for your loved one. Be careful about the

service you choose. Some of the best nursing facilities have a waiting list, and consequently, these
facilities usually do not deal with services. The service will not recommend these nursing facilities to
you because these facilities will not pay a referral
fee to the service. Also, some services do not visit
the nursing homes, so the service may be recom-
mending a facility they have never investigated.

If you prefer to find a nursing home on your
own, speak with doctors and nurses to get their
recommendations. Call the best hospitals in the
area, speak with the social worker, and ask for a
list of recommended nursing homes. Make certain that the facility can accommodate your loved
one's needs. Give scenarios—just as you did when
you were hiring the caregiver.

Generally, skilled nursing care is available only
for a short period of time after a hospitalization.
Custodial care is available for a much longer period. If a facility offers both types of care, learn
if residents may transfer between levels of care
within the nursing home without having to move
from their old room or from the nursing home.

Nursing homes that only take Medicaid residents might offer longer term but less intensive

levels of care. Nursing Homes that do not accept Medicaid may make a resident move when Medicare or the resident's own money runs out.

An occupancy rate is the total number of residents currently living in a nursing home divided by the home's total number of beds. Occupancy rates vary by area, depending on the overall number of available nursing home beds.

Take a tour of the facility. Ask if you may return at a different time unannounced to visit the facility. Make sure that the facility is open at all times for you and your family once your loved one is in the facility. After you see the rooms, ask to see the shower/bath where your loved one will be bathed.

Visit at mealtime. Sometimes the food a home serves is fine, but a resident still will not eat. Nursing home residents may like some control over their diet.

The Department of Health Services requires that a nursing facility provide a nurse calling system in all rooms and bathrooms so residents can ask for help at any time. Make sure that the call cord button will be within your loved one's reach. The nursing facility must respond to calls for assistance in a timely manner. If they cannot respond immediately, they need to inform you of that reason and let you know when they will assist you. They must be courteous when responding to your loved one and items must be within reach of your loved one.

Does the nursing facility assist with dressing, grooming, eating, moving, arranging transportation, sending mail, and receiving mail? Check with your local state department to determine the requirements in your state. Read all the paperwork given to you by the nursing facility. Find out exactly who would be taking care of your loved one. Request the gender of the caregiver, if desired. Choose a facility located near a family member so you have easy access to the facility.

"Nursing Home Compare," available on the internet at http://www.medicare.gov, provides summary information about every Medicare- and Medicaid-certified nursing home in the country. The website also contains information reported by the nursing homes prior to the last state inspection, including nursing home and resident characteristics. If you have questions or concerns about the information on a nursing home, discuss it during your visit. This chapter contains a questionnaire that you may want to ask the nursing home staff, family members and residents of the nursing home during your visit.

Bring a copy of the "Nursing Home Compare" inspection results for the nursing home. Ask whether the deficiencies have been corrected.

Ask to see a copy of the most recent nursing home inspection report.

Contact the Department of Health and request an overall report for the facility for the last three years. This is public information. Thoroughly review the report to better understand the level of care the patients receive, the cleanliness of the facility and its employees, and other valuable information that you should know before you sign any admitting papers.

> *My Experience*
> ## Nursing Homes
>
> I visited a highly reputable nursing facility and discovered feces everywhere in the wash area. The director became very flustered and attempted to assure me that this was just a rare mistake. Most people do not ask to see this part of the nursing facility.

Caring, competent nurses who respect each resident and family member are very important in assuring that residents get needed care and enjoy the best possible quality of life. Adequate nursing staff is needed to assess resident needs, plan and give them care, and help them with eating, bathing, and other activities. Some residents (those who are more dependent in eating or who are bedfast) need more help than other residents, depending on their conditions.

The combinations of registered nurses (RNs), licensed practical nurses (LPNs), vocational nurses (LVNs), and certified nursing assistants (CNAs) that a nursing home may have varies depending on the type of care that residents need and the number of residents in the nursing home. While the number of nursing staff is important to good care, also consider other factors, such as education and training.

Nursing Home Questionnaire

The following questionnaire can help you evaluate each nursing home you visit.

Name of Facility: _____

Head Administrator: _____

Address: _____

Phone Number: _____

Date of visit: _____

Licensing

■ Is the nursing home and the current administrator licensed by the state to operate?

■ What kind of licenses have these caregivers been issued?

■ Does the home conduct background checks on all staff?

■ Do the nursing home's procedures to screen potential employees for a history of abuse meet your state's requirements? Your state's Ombuds-

> *My Experience*
> ## Not Enough Help
>
> I wanted to place Marilyn in a nursing facility close to our home. We heard great things about it. We got Marilyn on the waiting list. We weren't allowed to tour the facility until Marilyn was accepted. We waited and waited. When Marilyn was finally accepted, we learned that the ratio of caregivers to patients was one to twelve. When I asked how often Marilyn would be bathed, I never received a concrete answer. My inner voice told me there was something wrong with this place, and I listened.

man program might be able to help you with this information.

■ Does the home have special services units, like rehabilitation, Alzheimer's, and hospice. Are there separate waiting periods or facility guidelines for when residents would be moved on or off the special unit?

■ Does the nursing home provide abuse prevention training?

■ What kind of training is required for the staff?

■ Do the nursing home's training programs educate employees about how to recognize resident abuse and neglect, how to deal with aggressive or difficult residents, and how to deal with the stress of caring for so many needs?

■ Are there clear procedures to identify events or trends that might lead to abuse and neglect, and procedures on how to investigate, report, and resolve your complaints?

■ Did I read the Health Report for the licensed facility?

■ What was the overall rating received by the nursing home?

■ Does that meet with my approval?

■ Do I have any questions to ask the administrators regarding the report?

ADMISSION

■ Can my loved one be admitted immediately?

■ If no, is there a waiting list?

■ Can my loved one get on the waiting list?

■ How long will the wait be?

FINANCES

■ What is the cost for the nursing facility?

■ Is everything inclusive?

■ Are there "extra" charges?

- What additional charges may be incurred?
- What is the cost for each additional charge?
- Does the facility accept Medicare?
- Does the facility accept Medicaid?
- If my loved one is on Medicaid, does the facility offer a comparable level of care for Medicaid patients?
- How many different levels of care does the nursing home offer?
- If my loved one is on Medicare, must he share a room?
- If yes, with how many other people?
- If this facility does not accept Medicaid and we can no longer pay, will the facility force my loved one to move out?

VISITING

- When are the visiting hours?
- Am I permitted to take my loved one out of the facility for a few hours during the day?
- Overnight?

BATHING

- Are the bathing areas clean?
- What does the staff use to clean the bath area?

- Does the staff clean the bath area after each patient is bathed?
- How many times a week will my loved one be bathed and shampooed?
- May I request additional days?
- Is there an additional fee for additional baths or showers?
- Does my loved one have to be bathed by a certain time?
- Do you provide and apply moisturizing lotion for the patients?
- If no, if we provide you with moisturizing lo-

My Experience

Second to Nun

Our Monsignor recommended an amazing nursing home run by nuns. I was very skeptical at first and interrogated the nuns. They could not believe the questions I had for them. I visited the facility several times before I admitted Marilyn. I examined many rooms and interviewed the patients and visitors. I spoke to many people and only received rave reviews.

The nuns treated Marilyn with dignity and kindness. On weekends, I had a private caregiver take Marilyn out to lunch, the movies, and our home.

tion, would your nurses be willing to apply the lotion to my loved one daily?

Nurses

■ How many registered nurses (RNs) are on the staff, and how many are available on each shift?

■ What is the patient to caregiver ratio?

■ Is a nurse call system in all rooms I visited?

■ If not, what was the director's response when I asked why they do not have a nurse call system?

■ How long does a patient have to wait before the nurse responds to the call system?

■ Are nursing staff members courteous and friendly to residents and to other staff?

■ Does the nursing staff respond in a timely manner to residents' calls for assistance, such as help getting in and out of bed, dressing, and going to the bathroom?

■ Which nursing staff members are involved in planning the residents' individual care? Are they the same ones who provide the care to residents?

■ Is there frequent turnover among certified nursing assistants (CNAs), nurses (RNs), supervisors, the Director of Nursing, or the Administrator? If yes, why?

■ What kind of training do certified nursing assistants (CNAs) receive?

■ How does the nursing home ensure that all staff receive continuing education and keep their knowledge and skills up-to-date?

CLOTHES AND LAUNDRY

■ Will I have to buy a specific type of clothing for my loved one?

■ Do you do the laundry for my loved one?

■ If yes, is this included in the base cost?

■ If no, how much more is it for this service?

■ Do you label the clothing for my loved one?

FACILITIES

■ Is the nursing home a non-smoking or smoking facility?

- Does my loved one need to bring her own furniture to the nursing home?
- Is my loved one permitted to have a television in her room?

QUALITY OF LIFE

- Can residents make choices about their daily routine, such as when to go to bed, get up, bathe, and eat?
- Is the interaction between staff and patient warm and respectful?
- Is the nursing home convenient and easy for friends and family to visit?
- Does the nursing home meet my loved one's cultural, religious, and language needs?
- Does the nursing home smell fresh, look clean, and have good lighting?
- Does the nursing home maintain comfortable temperatures?
- Do the resident rooms have personal articles and furniture?
- Do the public and resident rooms have comfortable furniture?
- Are the nursing home and its dining room generally quiet?

■ May residents choose from a variety of activities that they like?

■ Do outside volunteer groups visit the nursing home frequently?

■ Does the nursing home have pleasant outdoor areas for resident use, and does the staff help residents go outside?

■ How often are residents taken outside?

■ What time are the residents put to bed?

■ By what time are residents dressed in the morning and out of their rooms?

■ What activities does the nursing home offer for my loved one?

- Can we have a copy of the nursing home's monthly schedule of activities?
- Does the nursing home schedule outside activities for the residents?
- If I have a complaint regarding my loved one, what is the complaint process?
- If I send mail to my loved one, what is the procedure for delivery in this facility?

QUALITY OF CARE

- May residents continue to consult with their personal physician?
- Are residents clean, appropriately dressed, and well-groomed?
- Does the nursing home have an emergency medical system?
- Does the nursing home staff respond quickly to requests for help?
- Does the administrator and staff seem comfortable with each other and with the residents?
- Do residents have the same caregivers on a daily basis?
- Is there enough staff at night and on weekends or holidays to care for each resident?
- Does the home have an arrangement for emer-

> *My Experience*
> ## Food for Thought
>
> Caregivers in some nursing facilities are frequently told that they have a limited amount of time to feed each patient. If the patient does not eat fast enough, the food is thrown away and the caregiver moves on to the next patient. Sometimes if a patient refuses to cooperate, the caregiver gives the patient a cold shower as punishment. The caregiver might not change the adult diapers on patients for more than four hours. The management threatens to fire the caregivers unless they comply with the abusive practices.

gency situations with a nearby hospital?

■ Does the facility offer any services such as rehabilitation?

■ Are the family and resident councils independent from the nursing home's management?

■ Are care plan meetings held at convenient times for residents and their concerned family members to attend?

NUTRITION AND HYDRATION

■ Do you have a dietician on duty in the facility at all times?

- Will someone be monitoring my loved one's food intake?
- Can I request specific foods for my loved one?
- Can I request that certain foods not be given to my loved one?
- If my loved one is diabetic or becomes diabetic, will the facility provide a diabetic meal for my loved one?
- How much time does my loved one have to eat her meals?
- Is the dining time restricted?
- Is there enough staff to assist each resident who requires help with eating?
- If residents need help eating, do care plans specify what type of assistance they will receive?
- Does the food smell and taste good, and is it served at proper temperatures?
- Are residents offered a variety of food choices at mealtimes?
- Can residents select their meals from a menu or select their mealtime?
- Are water pitchers and drinking glasses provided on tables in the rooms?
- Does the staff help residents drink if they are not able to do so on their own?

- Are nutritious snacks available during the day and evening?
- Is each resident's weight routinely monitored?
- Does the environment in the dining room encourage residents to relax, socialize, and enjoy their food?
- Are residents rushed through meals or do they have time to finish eating and to use the meal as an opportunity to socialize with each other?
- Does the medicine a resident takes affect what they eat and how often they may want something to drink?

SAFETY

- Are there handrails in the hallways and grab bars in the bathrooms?
- Are the exits clearly marked?
- Are spills and accidents cleaned up quickly?
- Are hallways free of clutter and well lighted?
- Is there enough staff to help move residents quickly in an emergency?
- Does the nursing home have smoke detectors and sprinklers?
- Are there policies or procedures to safeguard resident possessions?

Restraints

■ Is there sufficient staff to assist residents who need help in moving or getting in and out of chairs and bed?

■ Who is involved in making the decisions about physical restraints?

■ When physical restraints are used, does the staff remove the physical restraints on a regular basis to help residents with moving and with activities of daily living?

■ Does the staff help residents with physical restraints to move as much as they would like to?

Bed Sores

■ How does the staff identify if a resident is at risk for skin breakdown?

■ What does the staff do to prevent bed sores for these residents?

■ What percentage of the residents have bed sores and why?

■ Do I see staff members helping residents change their positions in wheelchairs, chairs, and beds?

Incontinence

■ Does the nursing home smell clean?

■ What steps does the staff take to prevent bowel and bladder incontinence for those residents who are at risk?

DEPENDENCE IN EATING

■ Observe residents who need help in eating. Are they able to finish their meals or is the food returned to the kitchen uneaten?

■ Do all residents who need assistance with eating get help?

■ Does the staff give each resident enough time to chew food thoroughly and complete the meal?

BEDFAST

■ How are staff assigned to care for these residents who are bedfast?

RESTRICTED JOINT MOTION

■ How does the nursing home care for residents with restricted joint motion?

■ Do the residents get help with getting out of chairs and beds when they want to get up?

BEHAVIORAL SYMPTOMS

■ What management and/or medical approaches

does the nursing home use to treat behavioral symptoms?

■ How does staff handle residents that have behavioral symptoms such as calling out or yelling?

■ Are residents with behavioral symptoms checked by a doctor or behavioral specialist?

■ Does the staff receive special training to help them provide appropriate care to residents with behavioral symptoms?

Board and Care

While Assisted Living Facilities house hundreds of residents, Board and Care facilities take in only a few patients and provide caregivers around the clock. You will need to evaluate your loved one's situation to determine what kind of care is right for your loved one. When touring a Board and Care Facility, ask the same questions from the questionnaire.

Interview the owner of the Board and Care and investigate his background. Find out what kind of screening process he uses for his employees. Determine whether the employees are companions, RNs, or CNAs. Ask how long each employee has been working at the Board and Care. Speak with other residents to see if they like the facility. Make sure the facility can handle your loved one's needs. Find out the caregiver to patient ratio. Check the Health Report and make sure the facility and its administrator have a valid license.

Hospice

Hospice is a program that your loved one can be placed on if she is terminally ill and has approximately six months to live. This program provides nursing care in the home and pain medications if needed for comfort. Your doctor must sign the papers to make your loved one eligible for hospice. If you suspect that your loved has only a few months to live, sign up immediately. Do not wait until the last minute when your loved one is in pain. In most states, you can sign up six months before the individual is expected to die. Contact your local Medicare office to determine if Medicare will cover the cost of this program.

Chapter 11
TAKING CARE OF THE CAREGIVER

If you are not physically and emotionally well, you will not be able to properly care for your loved one. Oftentimes family members will take it upon themselves to do everything for their loved one without the help of others. You need to accept help from your family and friends. After some time doing everything yourself, you will start to resent not only your family but your ill loved one. This resentment will lead to depression, stress, and exhaustion—causing caregiver burnout.

Unfortunately, you will find that some family members will not want to deal with the situation at all. You may need to get respite care. This is assistance from other people to stay with your loved one to give you a break.

If you are the caregiver:

> *My Experience*
> ## Give Me a Break
>
> I noticed that one of the caregivers looked exhausted and needed a break. Marilyn's alter-ego "Skippy" would surface frequently and could be very harrowing. I told the caregiver to take a nap while I stayed with Marilyn. That one-hour break really helped reinvigorate the caregiver for the rest of the day. If I noticed the caregiver showing signs of stress, I would give the caregiver a break by taking Marilyn out myself for an hour.

■ See your doctor on a regular basis and test for stress and or depression.

■ Eat a well-balanced diet.

■ Be sure to get plenty of sleep.

■ Exercise on a regular basis. Walking is a great way to relieve stress.

■ Involve yourself in an activity solely for your own enjoyment. Join a social group, a church or synagogue, take up painting, or learn the piano.

■ Join a caregiver support group. Talking with people who are experiencing exactly what you are going through will boost your spirits and give you new ideas and resources.

■ Keep a journal. Write down your feelings on a daily basis so you can look back and evaluate your feelings and experiences—both negative and positive.

When A Loved One Dies

The death of a loved one can be a very difficult time. If your loved one had his will or trust in order, things will be easier. However, if there is no will or trust, you may face a very long probate proceeding.

When a loved one dies, the family should come together and decide on the funeral arrangements if that has not already been taken care of.

Do not be surprised if a caregiver starts asking you for your loved one's furniture, jewelry, personal belongings, clothing, shoes, etc. Some caregivers will believe that they are entitled to the belongings. Some caregivers will even tell you that your loved one promised them the item(s) they are requesting. I have had this happen to me, and I have spoken with many people who have had the same experience. If your loved one left valuables or objects with sentimental value in her home, do not be surprised to discover them missing. When you are in a state of grief, the caregiver may take what she feels is hers to take or whatever she was promised by your loved one. If something has sentimental value to you, remove it immediately before your loved passes away.

Remind the caregivers that they signed a job description and that the job description states that they are forbidden to accept gifts from your loved one.

Chapter 12
PAYING THE BILLS

Some people can get financial assistance from Medicare. For instance, in California, Medicare will assist in paying for in-home health care. Medicare requires that you meet the following criteria to qualify for this program:

■ Your loved one's doctor must request the program and start an in-home health care plan for you.

■ Your loved one must be homebound, meaning he cannot leave his home to go to the doctor.

■ Medicare must approve the home health care company you choose.

■ Your loved one must need skilled nursing care, physical therapy, or language pathology services.

Medicare can also assist with covering Social Care services, medical supplies, and equipment. In the state of California, there is a 20 percent deductible for equipment.

Medicaid helps individuals with a low income or no income. This person can qualify for several programs offered through Medicare such as prescriptions and hospital bills. Call a Medicare office near you, tell the representative your situation, and ask for all of the options available for your loved one.

Bibliography

- *Taking Care of Tomorrow: A Consumer's Guide to Long-Term Care* (California Department of Aging, 1998)
- *Losing a Million Minds—Disease and Other Dementias* (Washington, D.C.: U.S. Congress, Office of Technology Assessment, April 1987))
- *Caregiver Stress* (Alzheimer's Association, 1987)
- http://ombudsman.lacounty.gov

Resources

Alzheimer's Association National Office
919 Michigan Avenue, Suite 1000
Chicago, IL 60611-1676
Tel: (312) 335-8700
24/7 Helpline: (800)-272-3900
http://www.alz.org

Family Caregiver Alliance
Statewide Clearinghouse on Brain Impairments
   and Caregiver Issues
425 Bush Street, Suite 500
San Francisco, CA 94108
Tel: (415) 434-3388
http://www.caregiver.org

National Association for Continence
P.O. Box 1019
Union, SC 29402-1019
Tel: (843) 377-0900; (800) BLADDER
http://www.nafc.org

Los Angeles Caregiver Resource Center
3120 N. Clybourn Ave
Burbank, CA 91505
Tel: (818) 847-9141; (800) 540-4442
http://lacrc.usc.edu

National Stroke Association
9707 East Easter Lane, Suite B
Centennial, CO 80112-3747
Tel: (303) 649-9299; (800) 787-6537
http://www.stroke.org

Acknowledgments

I am grateful to my husband, Jay, and my three beautiful girls, Alexandra, Samantha and Jacqueline, for always being there to bring a smile to my face when I've had a hard day; my mother for always helping me whenever I needed her; my sister, Carol, for being there for me day and night and never wanting anything in return, and to Brice for his understanding; my brother, Charly, and his family, who have always been there to support me; my sister-in-law, Hilaire, for being my partner in detective work, and her husband, Todd, for his support; Dick Block, without whom nothing was possible; Joan Kievman, Marilyn's best friend, who was always there for Marilyn; Dr. Bruce Miller at the UCSF Memory and Aging Center for treating Marilyn with dignity and for always going out of his way to help our family; Dr. Peter Grossman at the Grossman Burn Center for the care and compassion he gave Marilyn; Monsignor Paul Dotson for always being there for our family; Judy Bogen, my rock and the best attorney in town; and the nuns at Mary Health of the Sick for the amazing kindness you showed Marilyn and our family.

www.ingramcontent.com/pod-product-compliance
Lightning Source LLC
Chambersburg PA
CBHW030515100426
42813CB00001B/48